CW00951868

WILMSLOW and ALDERLEY EDGE

Quarry Bank Mill & Manchester Airport

A Pictorial History

Macclesfield Hundred, from Speed's Map of Cheshire, 1610.

WILMSLOW and ALDERLEY EDGE

Quarry Bank Mill & Manchester Airport

A Pictorial History

Roy Westall

Phillimore

1994

Published by
PHILLIMORE & CO. LTD.,
Shopwyke Manor Barn, Chichester, West Sussex

ISBN 0 85033 867 0

Printed and bound in Great Britain by
BIDDLES LTD.
Guildford, Surrey

*This book is dedicated to
the late
Jack Robinson
a friend*

List of Illustrations

Frontispiece: Section from Speed's Map of Cheshire, 1610

Acknowledgements

I would like to offer my thanks to Manchester Airport Archives, Quarry Bank Trust, and both Wilmslow and Alderley Edge libraries for kindness in allowing me access to their photographic archives and for their generosity in giving me permission to reproduce the following photographs: Manchester Airport Archives, 119-127, 129-31, 133-34, 136, 190 and the photocopies from the opening ceremony; Quarry Bank Trust, 57, 59-84, 86-9, 93, 100-11; Alderley Edge library, 142, 144, 148, 153, 160, 172, 174, 180, 181, 183, 185; Wilmslow library, 3, 5, 6, 9-12, 15-17, 20-36, 38-40, 42-49, 50-56, 143, 145-47, 150, 152, 155, 161, 164, 168, 177.

I would also like to thank Janet Maynard for her help in checking the text of this book, and the following for their kindness in allowing me to reproduce their photographs: *Express Advertiser & Times* Group of Newspapers (Stockport), and their photographer Chris Hill, 135; Gerry and Annie Devine of the *George and Dragon*, Wilmslow, 14, 37; The Guardian newspapers, 132; Brian Hobson, 178; The Imperial War Museum, 127, 131; Basil Jeuda, 13, 149, 150-1, 163; Manchester Evening News, 128; The Manchester Museum (University of Manchester), 41, 162; the following photographs were taken by Roy Westall, 4, 8, 58, 85, 92, 94-99, 154, 156, 157, 159, 165-67, 169-71, 173, 175, 179, 182, 184, 188, 189, 191-96.

Wilmslow

Introduction

It has been suggested that the name 'Wilmslow' derives from Wighelmes-hlaw, -hlaw being the early pagan name for a burial mound. This would fit in with the fact that, during the excavation of railway cuttings near the station in 1839, an urn containing cremated remains, together with an early bronze-age dagger, was found. Twenty years later a second urn was found nearby. John Earwaker records the event:

> The spot where the urn was found is about one hundred yards distant from Wilmslow railway station, in a ridge of gravel between the new and the old roads leading to the village of Presbury ... the bones are much chared, and show evident traces of the action of fire. The teeth are nearly perfect and appear to be those of a young person about 14 years of age.

Strange though it may seem, the ancient parish of Wilmslow had no township with its name until 1894, when the townships of Bollin Fee, Chorley, Fulshaw and Pownall Fee were combined to create Wilmslow civil parish, which, at that time, had a population of 4,296. Prior to that date, the place name 'Wilmslow' referred only to the area on which stood the parish church of St Bartholomew.

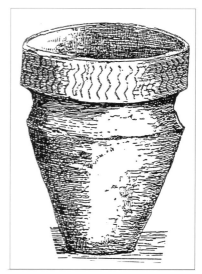

1 A drawing of the urn found at Wilmslow in 1859.

Wilmslow parish church

The parish church at Wilmslow is dedicated to St Bartholomew and is situated in the lowest part of the town adjacent to the river Bollin. It was first mentioned in the year 1246, in the *inquisitions post mortem* of Sir Richard Fitton, who held the manor of Bolyn. In the early part of the 16th century the church was remodelled, leaving little of the medieval building. A brass memorial to Robert Dunham and his lady, dated 1460, is set into the chancel floor and is the earliest to be found in Cheshire. The base of the tower is thought to be of similar age. The graveyard is noted for quite a number of old slabs; one, bearing the date 1596, commemorates the burial of the children of Thomas Dale.

There is evidence from the churchwardens' accounts that St Bartholomew's was also being used as a school as early as 1587. The accounts commence in 1585, in the middle of the reign of Elizabeth I, shortly after the rebuilding of the church. They give a fascinating glimpse into life in late 16th- and early 17th-century rural England.

It was the duty of the church elders to provide help to the needy, and the church porch was looked upon as an asylum for destitute and poor strangers who were seeking relief. In 1598 the sum of 4d. was paid 'For removing and relieving a poore woman in the church porch and for dressing it' whilst in 1612 the sum of 12d. was given to a poor man of Knutsford after his smithy had burnt down.

Plague was not unknown and the entry for 19 May 1658 says that this was 'a day set aprt for (to) humble ourselves in prayer, fasting and preachings for the sore affliction w(hich) is upon the nation by soe many being visited and many dieing, which summe so collected was nyne shillings and one penny'. The money collected was distributed to the poor.

Like many buildings today, the church was having problems with pigeon droppings, and one can imagine the mirth and guffaws from the peasantry when the 'target' was a lady's bonnet or best gown. In 1670, 4s. 8d. was 'Paid for a new door to set up in the top of the steeple to keepe forth the Piggens from fowleinge the church'. Obviously this did not work, for five years later one shilling was 'paid for a nette to keep the Pigeons forth of ye Church'. However this also failed to keep these pests away, and in 1678, in apparent desperation, 2d. was 'spent for shotte and powder to kill the pigeons in the church'.

In 1863 St Bartholomew's underwent major restoration which did not meet with universal approval. Robert Langton, complaining about the loss of its ancient character, wrote to the Lancashire and Cheshire Antiquarian Society:

This church was altered—I cannot call it restored—in 1863. It must have had then certainly a venerable appearance—something old, wild, and quaint, you will say! It took some £7,000 to convert this old building into a spic and span bran *(sic)* new looking church. A very short description of the alteration must suffice. In the first place, a score or two of dead bodies were removed to make room for a transeptal chapel, with heating apparatus beneath. The plain oak timbered roofs of the aisles of the nave were panelled with deal at £1 a panel; a chancel arch was built where no chancel arch was ever seen before; the ancient seats of solid oak, the first benches ever placed in the nave of the church, and which had existed for a century or two under the seats, which were a more modern but still old set of pews, were removed; many of the monuments altogether disappeared, including some to the memory of the Trafford family; painted benefiction boards were removed from the walls and placed behind the organ boards, like 'benefits forgot'; the ancient font was shifted into the churchyard, and replaced by a very poor new one; and lastly, when the church was re-opened, the old parishioners, mostly farmers, were put into the cold, while a new set of people mostly from the large houses of Alderley Edge, were installed in the best places in the church.

2 This drawing shows Wilmslow church shortly after major restoration in 1863.

3 This photograph of St Bartholomew's was taken in the latter part of the 19th century. In 1903 the lychgate was added.

4 For a short period of time the church was influenced by puritan doctrine and in 1642 the ornate baptismal font was sold, being replaced with a simple pewter basin. With the crowning of Charles II in 1660, the situation was reversed and 17s. 6d. was spent on this new, and more decorative font.

5 Church Street at the turn of the century. The town pump can be seen on the right.

6 Church Street looking north at the turn of the century.

Highways

The industrial revolution brought with it a new generation of 'middle class' people who needed an efficient transport system to take them from the small villages and emerging towns to the centres of commerce such as Manchester, Birmingham and London. They pressed the government to allow them to improve existing roads or to build new ones.

In order to pay for and maintain these privately-built turnpike roads, toll-gates were introduced and it was normal for a fee to be levied on all vehicles and animals that used them. As travelling the King's Highway had been free for centuries, many folk thought that it should remain so. Armed gangs often took the law into their own hands, knocked down gates, damaged the toll-houses and attacked the keepers.

7 These coaches of the time of Charles II demonstrate the problems of passing on unmade roads.

8 After passing through Wilmslow, packhorses laden with salt would have crossed this bridge at Bollington on their way to Yorkshire.

9 Wilmslow had two tollbars, one being at Fulshaw Cross. This view, taken in the early 1900s, shows Alderley Road looking towards Wilmslow Road. The toll charge of '2d. for a vehicle of any sort' was abolished in 1873.

Travellers from Manchester to Congleton would pass through Wilmslow via what are now Cliff Road, Chancel Lane, Church Road, Bank Square and Grove Street. In the second half of the 18th century it was suggested that the roads should be widened and improved to make it possible for mail coaches to enter the village. However with opposition from residents who feared that the churchyard would be disturbed, a new road was built parallel to it. Prior to the opening of Manchester Road in 1775, Wilmslow Bridge was constructed to take it over the Bollin. Manchester Road became one of the main coach roads to London and, in order to cater for the needs of the traveller, a whole network of hostelries developed, providing a meal and a bed for the night, as well as a fresh team of horses for the coachman.

According to Pigot's *Commercial Directory* of 1834, the *Swan* was the main coaching inn at Wilmslow, and from here transport could be obtained to:

BIRMINGHAM, the Royal Mail (from Manchester) every day at twelve—the 'Eclipse' every morning at a quarter before eight.

MANCHESTER, the 'Royal Mail' (from Birmingham) every day at twelve—the 'Eclipse' every afternoon at four—and a market coach (the Velocipede) every Tuesday and Saturday morning at half-past seven.

One of the first recorded road accidents in the area happened on 20 January 1818 when Joseph Crumbleholme of Manchester, aged 18, was killed 'in consequence of the accidental overturning of the mailcoach'.

10   Manchester Road, showing the new road on the left and the old road on the right. St Bartholomew's can be seen in the distance.

11 Manchester Road (new) looking towards the Bollin at the turn of the century.

12 It was the opening of the Manchester-Crewe railway line in 1842 that transformed the villages of Wilmslow and Alderley Edge into high-class residential areas. This photograph shows the construction of the line.

13 Wilmslow station, *c*.190
The coal yard on the left w
later moved to the other side
the road, and the bridge w
replaced a few years later.

14 In order to accommodate the new visitors
to Wilmslow, William Warham built the
Railway Hotel on Station Road in 1860.

15 This view was taken in th
early 1900s, and shows Statio
Road looking towards Ban
Square and Swan Street.

Romany of the B.B.C.

One of the town's best known inhabitants was the naturalist 'Romany of the B.B.C.', as the Rev. George Bramwell Evans was known. He came to Wilmslow in 1939, seeking a peaceful retirement, but unfortunately the week he arrived saw the outbreak of the Second World War. He was recruited by the B.B.C. and so for the next four years G.B. Evans broadcast on children's hour.

In 1921 he had purchased a gypsy caravan for his holidays, having gleaned an interest in roaming the countryside from his mother, Tilly Smith, a born gypsy. His caravan often featured in many of his books and radio programmes, and so realistic were his tales of rural life that the majority of his listeners did not realise that he was speaking from a studio.

Following Romany's death on 20 November 1943, aged 59, the caravan was presented to Wilmslow U.D.C. by his widow, and thousands of his fans came to see it.

16 In 1950 Wilmslow council opened this garden in memory of Romany.

17 Tilly Smith, the gypsy mother of Romany.

Trade and Industry

The manufacture of gloves, mohair yarn and silk stitched and capped buttons represented the traditional industries of Wilmslow, though by the early part of the 18th century there were six cotton mills and one silk mill in the village. Two of these cotton mills stood on ground near the river, which now forms part of the churchyard.

Pigot's *Commercial Directory* for Wilmslow shows that in 1834 there were a number of traders working in the village including boot and shoe makers (2), butchers (4), dressmaker (1), druggist (1), ironmonger (1), plumbers and glaziers (2), retailer of beer (1), saddlers (2), shopkeepers and dealers in sundries (7), tailors (4) and drapers (2).

Whilst the village blacksmith, John Sidebotham, maintained the welfare of the horses, Joseph Dean, Thomas Moore and Joseph Nightingale looked after the welfare of the residents, all three being surgeons.

There were 12 pubs within the parish of Wilmslow at this time, keeping the population of 4,973 in liquid refreshment. Those in Wilmslow village were the *Bull's Head*, the *George & Dragon*, the *King William*, the *New Inn*, the *Ring of Bells* and the *Swan Inn*.

Writing in 1923, Charles Prince says that

> there are some fine shops in Wilmslow and that the General Post Office is situated in Hawthorn Lane, whilst the County Police Building and the new Roman Catholic Church are in Green Lane. In Grove Street can be found the District Council Offices, the British Workman's Hall, and the Conservative Club whilst the Comrades Club and several banks stand in Bank Square.
>
> The Drill Hall, Gas Works, and Parish Church are down Church Street, together with the Market Ground where a market is held every Friday.

TELEPHONE 348.

JACKSONS (WILMSLOW) LTD.

REMOVALS. HAULAGE.

CHAR-A-BANCS AND PRIVATE CARS.

LOWEST POSSIBLE RATES QUOTED.

PHONE 354.

FOR ECONOMY, EFFICIENCY WITH COURTESY—

ROBERT JAFFREY,

SANITARY ENGINEER AND DECORATOR,

SOLE ADDRESS: HAWTHORN ST., WILMSLOW

SOLICITS YOUR ESTEEMED ENQUIRIES.

ADVICE AND ESTIMATES FREE.

TELEPHONE 4 X.   ESTABLISHED 1864.

C, CHARNLEY,

Dispensing Chemist,

The Grove Pharmacy, Wilmslow.

Surgical and Nursing Requisites.   Photographic Materials and Chemicals.

Schweppes & Ellis's Aerated Waters.   Stranges A1 Crystal Oil.

H. NORBURY,

Pianoforte and Music Dealer

Gramophones, Records.   Tuning and Repairs.

STATION ROAD, WILMSLOW.

18 Adverts for removals, decorator, chemist and music dealer dating from 1923.

19 This advertisement for a house in Holly Road appeared in 1938 and is typical of those built for wealthy Manchester businessmen.

QUALITY HOUSES
by
Gibson
'HOLWOOD'
HOLLY ROAD
WILMSLOW
1009

20 Silk Mill Cottage, 1930s. The mill stood in the area known as the Carrs, but with the decline of the silk industry it was converted into a calico printing factory.

21 This view of a corn mill *(centre)* and the parish church *(top right)* was taken from Wilmslow viaduct, *c*.1920.

22 The old silk mill in the Carrs.

23 Market gardening was once a major industry in the Wilmslow area. These people are binding rhubarb. The picture dates from 1917.

24 These market gardeners were photographed in 1910 whilst on their way to work in Moss Nook.

25 Looking towards Church Street from Bank Square at the turn of the century.

26 Taken in the early 1900s from Bank Square, this photograph shows Hawthorn Lane on the left and Swan Street on the right.

27 In 1858 Walter Shields Craig established his firm of drapers and outfitters, seen here in 1905 on the corner of Hawthorn Street and Church Street. A century later the company was still in business as a fashion store, restaurant and funeral directors. In 1910 W.S. Clegg and his son W.T. Clegg were offering after hours and Sunday deliveries for urgent orders. So much for the Sunday Trading Act.

28 It was traditional for northern mill towns to close for a week to enable the workers to have a holiday. Wakes week, as they were known, derived from the commemoration of the dedication of the parish church. This photograph, taken during Wakes week in 1913, shows the Wilmslow carnival parading along Swan Street from Bank Square. The Public Hall Picture House can be seen on the right.

29 Where has all the traffic gone? This village image of Swan Street was taken in the late 19th century. The man on the left appears to be delivering milk.

30 An interesting picture of higgledy-piggledy buildings on Green Lane. From the style of the car it would seem that the picture was probably taken during the 1930s or '40s.

31   Grove Street, looking towards Bank Square at the turn of the century.

This picture shows the Conservative Club and Mark Wood's shop festooned for the coronation of King George V 1911.

33 Pedestrians and cyclists pose for this photograph of Grove Street, decorated for the coronation of King George V in 1911.

34   Grove Street from Bank Square in the 1930s.

35 The Ardern family appear to have been trading in Wilmslow for a long time. In 1834 William Ardern had a shop here, and by 1874 Job Ardern was established on Grove Street as a glass, china and general dealer, as well as being a pianoforte tuner. This photograph of his glass and earthernware store on Grove Street was taken *c*.1906. By 1928 the company had been taken over by Job's executors.

36   Another trader on Grove Street was Johnson's Saddler and Harness Maker, seen here in the early 1900s. John Edward Johnson and sons appear to have adapted their business to meet the needs of a more popular means of transport—the bicycle. In 1906 they were trading as saddle and bicycle makers and in 1934 they advertised themselves only as cycle manufacturers.

37 The original fire station stood on Swan Street where this photograph of a horse-drawn engine was taken in the late 19th century. A new fire-station was opened at Little Lindow on Altrincham Road in 1962.

Punishment

An act passed in 1650 specified that 'any person convicted of profane swearing or cursing, on the oath of one witness, shall pay, if a Duke or Lord, 30s.; if a Baronet or Knight, 20s.; an Esquire, 10s.; a Gentleman, 6s. 8d.; every other person, 3s. 4d.'

On 20 December 1659, two men of the parish of Wilmslow were fined a total of 20s. for being drunk and swearing. The money was sent to the churchwarden for distribution amongst the poor.

In 1656 the churchwarden paid 10s. for the four constables of Bollin Fee 'to bringe a women unto the house of correction'.

In 1773 a workhouse was erected on the Wilmslow side of Lindow Common facing the old racecourse, the land having been donated by freeholders. By the end of the 19th century it had been replaced by the Union Workhouse at Knutsford and the building had been converted into cottages. Gorsey Bank Primary School now occupies the site.

The introduction of new machinery in the latter part of the 18th century was putting people's livelihoods under threat, creating bitterness between employee and employer and between the indigenous population and Irish immigrants. With so many inns and no restrictions on drinking times, Wilmslow acquired a reputation for drunkenness and disorder.

However when the artist Samuel Finney (1719-98) retired to Fulshaw and became a Justice of the Peace, he devoted the remainder of his life to quelling the riots. He put down 'hooliganism' with such firmness that Wilmslow has wryly claimed a reputation for respectability ever since. Samuel Finney is buried at Wilmslow parish church.

38 This undated drawing shows the old lock-up or dungeon which stood on the west side of Church Street, on the site now occupied by Burton House. It was built in 1846 and contained two cells and a residence for the police constable, the first being Mr. James Garner.

39 Gorsey Bank School now occupies the site of Altrincham Road Workhouse, shown here at the beginning of the century.

The Racecourse and Lindow Moss

Races were held on the last week of August on what is now known as Racecourse Road. These were abandoned towards the end of the last century, following complaints that they damaged the neighbourhood.

The road surrounds an area known as Lindow Common, wherein lies Black Lake, formed in the late glacial period by the merging of sand-laden streams and melting blocks of ice.

As the ice age receded, vegetation began to grow in this wetland area, followed later by forests. Where drainage was impeded moss began to form, as it has continued to do to the present day. By late Roman times the woodland areas had been cleared and the region was used for mixed arable and pasture.

The Common was enclosed in 1777, later to be divided amongst the landowners of the parish. Historians have recorded that many disastrous fires occurred on the moss during dry summers, and that both men and cattle had sometimes been drowned in the treacherous bog. At one time vipers were so common that a viper-catcher came annually to catch them. They were described as being 'from 12 to 14 inches long, of the adder species, their bites poisonous and often fatal, but that the application of sweet oil was found to be a valuable remedy'. There is a record of a barefotted boy who had been bitten 'whilst gathering cranberries on the Common. Oil had been applied, and he was out of danger, but he had a very cadaverous look, and all the lower part of his body was much swollen and puffed up, and greatly disfigured with foul black and yellow colours, as if he had been sorely crushed and bruised. A pointer dog that was bitten in the head died within twelve hours'.

For centuries the turf here has been dried and sold for fuel. Modern machinery has enabled greater quantities to be removed annually than ever before and, perhaps more importantly, from a greater depth. This has led to a number of macabre finds.

40 Skaters take advantage of Black Lake in this winter scene taken early this century.

In 1983 a human head, thought to date from the Iron Age, was found. The following year the well-preserved body of a man was unearthed by a peat digger. He became a national celebrity overnight when it was discovered that he had been ritually killed. He had been struck twice on the head by a narrow bladed instrument with sufficient force to drive bone deep into the cranium. A thong neatly tied round his neck and a laceration to the right of the larynx suggests that garrotting and slitting of his throat may have completed this grisly ritual.

Carbon dating indicates that Pete (Peat) Marsh, as he became known, died about 2,700 years ago at the age of twenty-five. Originally he lay naked, face down in the water by the side of a shallow pool. From the evidence he was well built, had a neatly trimmed moustache and beard, together with manicured fingernails, and it would appear that he came from a wealthy background. His body is currently (1994) being exhibited in the British Museum.

41 This waxworks reconstruction of Lindow Man was made by Richard Neave of Manchester Museum.

42 A postcard of Black Lake on Lindow Common.

Wilmslow Life

43 Stephen Beswick was a well known local character in the late 19th century.

44 In the late 19th century 'Olde Wilmslowe' was another well known local character.

45 Rural Hawthorn Street in the middle of the 19th century.

46 Carnival parade in Hawthorn Street, *c*.1909.

47 *(Above left)* Founded towards the end of the 18th century, the old Methodist chapel, *(left)* stood on Water Lane in an area known as Little Venice. How Little Venice got its name is unknown, but Water Lane and Spring Street nearby may indicate that the area was subject to flooding.

48 *(Above right)* These old cottages once stood on Parsonage Green at the turn of the century.

49 A Sunday School procession parades down Water Lane in the late 19th century.

50 *(Right)* This delightful picture shows garland dancers on Carnival field, Altrincham Road, at the turn of the century. The field is still used for carnivals today.

51 *(Below left)* Photographed in 1910 at Wilmslow carnival, the children are dressed as characters from the fairy tale 'Little Red Riding Hood'.

52 *(Below right)* Wilmslow carnival in 1912.

nslow Carnival 1912. AE.

53 Pupils at the County School in 1912.

54 Pupils at Wilmslow Church of England Junior School in the late 19th century. The headteacher was Mrs. Singleton.

55 Morley Green School pupils in the 1890s. On the left is Miss Isobella Ashbrook, the first headmistress.

Styal Village

This pretty village of cobbled streets, black-and-white 'magpie' cottages, deep wooded valley, and historic mill is owned mainly by the National Trust but administered by the Quarry Bank Mill Trust Ltd., an independent charitable trust. Every year, thousands of school parties from all over the country visit Quarry Bank Mill and the surrounding estate to expand their knowledge of the industrial revolution andd the textile trade. However, being situated less than a mile from Manchester International Airport, the mill has often been under threat of demolition in order to construct a new runway. The village also houses Styal open prison, until recently a semi-secure women's prison but originally built as an orphanage known as 'The Cottage Homes'.

Styal, together with the hamlets of Morley and Stanilands, originally formed the township of Pownall Fee, part of the ancient parish of Wilmslow.

One of the earliest recording of 'the fee of Pownall' was in 1331 when John Fitton wrote:

> To all &c. John son of Edmund ffiton *(sic)* sends greeting. Know ye that I have let to farm to Hugh ffiton *(sic)*, parson to the Church of Wilmslowe, a piece of my land in Stiale in pounale for the erecting thereon a certain grange for the storing of the tenths of the corn of the said Hugh. To have and to hold from the feast of Pentacost anno dni M.CCC.xxxi, for twenty years free from rent.

56 Twinnies Bridge on the Carrs.

The site of this tythe barn is unknown but, close to Twinney Bridge, where the rivers Bollin and Dean meet, lie the remains of an old mill, believed to date from 1335, which may have been built to grind the corn stored in the nearby barn.

An 18th-century historian, Samuel Finney, claimed that a poor man of the parish named Murral lived with his wife and children in the cave near what is now the site of the river. They made it habitable by filling in the front with gorse to keep out the cold.

At Styal Green stood the village stocks and Styal Cross. Sometime during the 19th century the cross was moved to the junction of Holly Road and Altrincham Road where it stood until it was demolished by a car accident in the 1960s. The base and stump now stand in a safer place in the village.

57 *(Above)* This photograph shows Styal Cross, which, together with the village stocks, once stood at Styal Green.

58 *(Left)* The remains of the Cross now stand in a safer place in the village.

Samuel Greg and Quarry Bank Mill

The 18th century saw the manufacture of cotton cloth change from a cottage industry into a factory process. This had been brought about by an increase in plantations in the southern states of America, together with the invention of the spinning jenny, the flying shuttle, the spinning mule and the steam engine.

It was during this rapidly changing period that Samuel Greg came on the scene. Born in Belfast in 1758, he was one of 13 children, and from the age of 10 he was raised by two uncles who taught him the business of trading in cloth. When Samuel was 24 years of age his uncles died, leaving him the enormous sum of £22,000.

Deciding to invest his money by building a spinning mill, he came to Styal where he found a good water supply to power his mill, cheap land to rent, and nearby quarries where he could obtain building stone.

On 6 January 1784, Samuel Greg leased land known as Quarrell Hole 'for carrying on the trade of business of carding, roving, spinning, and manufacturing of cotton'. The landlord, Lord Stamford, stipulated that none of the trees surrounding the projected mill should be trimmed, lopped or felled, and hence the woodlands that can be seen today look much as they would have done when Samuel Greg first saw them.

By the 1830s the Gregs had become very wealthy. Samuel's eldest son, Thomas, became a landed gentleman, and the business had been taken over by his second son, Robert Hyde Greg, described as a 'stern, reserved and careful man' who had an uneasy relationship with his father. In 1831 Robert Hyde Greg built Norcliffe Hall and introduced deer onto his estate. Ironically, his father died in 1831 after a lingering illness, having been attacked by a stag. Samuel Greg was buried at Wilmslow church, where there is a mural tablet to his memory and to that of his wife.

For a short period of his life, Robert Hyde Greg became an M.P. for Manchester. In 1838 he planted many of the trees in the ravine, including cuttings of Wellingtonias *(Sequoiadendron giganteum)*, taken from 3,500-year-old trees in California. These parent trees have attained a height of 350 ft., as one day may their offspring. Robert Hyde Greg died on 21 February 1875 at the age of 80 and was buried at the Unitarian chapel, Dean Row. His funeral was attended 'by numerous employees and tenants, both at Styal and Reddish, nearly 500 in number, and many private friends'.

59 Prior to the Industrial Revolution, spinning and weaving was carried out at home.

60 A portrait of Samuel Greg, 1738-1834.

61 Samuel married Hannah Lightbody in 1789. This portrait dates from *c*.1800.

62 The original doorway to the mill. The inscription says 'Quarry Bank Mills, Built by Samuel Greg Esquire of Belfast Ireland anno domini 1784'.

63 This photograph shows the section of mill that was built in 1784, although the chimney was built a century later when steam power was introduced. The clock and bell tower were built in 1796 when the mill was further extended. Containing two bells, one rang at the start of the day, whilst the other would strike on the hour.

64 In 1796 Samuel Greg built Quarry Bank House for himself, his wife, Hannah, and their children. Situated adjacent to the mill, the house remains privately owned.

65 This was the mill manager's house. Built next to the mill, the manager was always 'on-call'.

66 Taken in 1906, this is thought to be the oldest photograph of the mill. In those days it was covered in ivy.

67 As part of the mill's bicentenary celebrations in 1984, these cotton bales were brought from America to Liverpool, and then transported to Styal by horse-drawn wagon, as had happened in 1784.

68 Quarry Bank Mill is visited by thousands of school parties every year. Here Jack Bromley demonstrates a power mule.

69 The river Bollin flows behind the mill. Samuel Greg dammed the river to drive his water wheel. As output increased, he installed a great wheel which had a diameter of over 50ft.

70 The weir on the river Bollin.

71 When a steam engine was installed in the late 19th century, the great wheel fell into disrepair. In the late 1980s Quarry Bank Trust installed this new one of similar size.

72 Built in the Jacobean style in 1834 by Robert Hyde Greg, this photograph of Norcliffe Hall was taken at the turn of the century. Externally it appears very much the same today.

73 Robert Hyde Greg in his youth.

74 Robert Hyde Greg aged seventy.

75 Mary, the wife of Robert Hyde Greg.

Greg's Estate

In the 18th century, Styal consisted of little more than three farms which were accessed via Lindow Common. Even the populations of the nearby towns of Stockport (15,000) and Manchester (22,000) were small, and, although in the beginning Samuel Greg managed to recruit women spinners from the neighbourhood, the first being a local girl named Penny Chapman, he soon had to look further afield.

The nearby farmsteads of Shaws Fold and Farm Fold contained ancient buildings which Samuel Greg adapted to accommodate his employees and their families. The 13th-century thatched farmhouse at Farm Fold was converted into three cottages, a Dutch barn converted into four cottages, a cruck-framed cottage divided into two, and at Shaw's Fold, a large barn was made into seven cottages.

The first purpose-built cottages were constructed in 1806 for the new migrant families, one of the first being the Venables, whose descendants still live in Styal. Four larger cottages were built in 1810 and 1822, and two sets of double row houses built. These developments were known as Oak Cottages. Each cottage contained two rooms up, two rooms down, a cellar, and a back yard with privy. Cellars were rented separately, often to ex-apprentices who wished to stay in the employment of the Gregs.

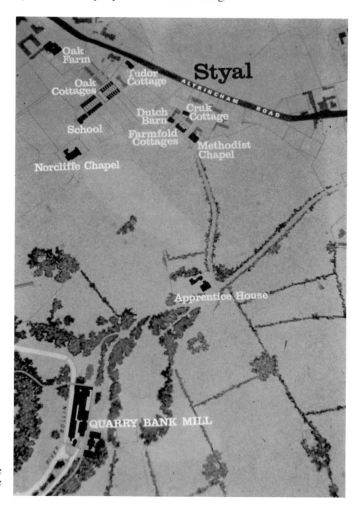

76 This map shows the estate of the Greg family. It now belongs to the National Trust.

77   Cottages at Shaw Fold.

78   These cottages at Farm Fold were originally a Dutch barn. On the right is the Methodist chapel, once a corn store.

79 This thatched cottage at Farm Fold is believed to date from the 13th century.

80 This building is known as Tudor Cottages. It dates from the time of Henry VIII.

81 In order that his employees could purchase fresh meat Greg rented Oak Farm. It was not until 1802 that he purchased the farm, which now belongs to the National Trust.

82 Oak Cottages. These were amongst the first purpose-built houses for mill workers.

83 How the inside of one of C Cottages would have appeared the first half of the 19th centu

The Village Shop

Pay was poor. A good female spinner could earn up to 7s. 6d. per week whilst a male weaver could earn 10s. per week. After deductions for rent and fines for stoppages, faults in the cloth, lateness etc., there was little left to feed the family. Like many mill-owners of the time, the Gregs paid their workers, not in cash, but in tokens or badges, which could only be spent at Greg's shop in the village.

Under the Truck Act of 1831, this system of payment was abolished, and the shop came under the management of the employees. A profit sharing scheme was introduced in the 1850s and in 1873 it was taken over by the newly-formed Styal Co-operative Society, later absorbed by the Stockport Society.

84 *(Left)* Opened in the early part of the 19th century, the shop, together with the rest Greg's estate, was handed over to the National Trust in 1939, but remained in use for the villagers until the 1970s. This photograph was taken in May 1965.

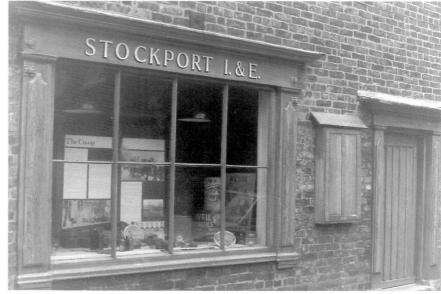

85 *(Right)* The village shop, 1993. Notice that the old door has been restored in the side of the building. The little cupboard at the side of the door contained a board on which any deceased villager could be laid.

Religion

Greg had been brought up as a Presbyterian whilst his wife, Hannah, had Unitarian convictions. The majority of his employees were either Baptist or Methodist. In order to provide for their religious needs the foundation stones of Norcliffe chapel were laid in 1822. There was great excitement amongst the Greg family, as Hannah Greg records:

> We all trouped down to the Oak Chapel to lay our brick. Everyone in the village could also lay a brick and the workmen had a little treat at night drinking the ladies health.

This place of worship was officially opened in 1823 as a Baptist chapel but is now used by the Unitarians. It still contains a full-size baptismal font, under the floor beneath the pulpit, which had to be filled every Saturday night, using buckets of water carried from the water pump near Oak Farm.

Followers of John and Charles Wesley, however, were by now becoming widespread throughout the village, and, in 1837, in order to satisfy their needs, Robert Hyde Greg gave permission to convert a corn-store in Farm-Fold into a Methodist chapel. It continues to serve this function today.

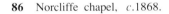

86 Norcliffe chapel, *c*.1868.

87 An old photograph of cottages at Farm Fold. The Methodist chapel stands at the end of the row.

88 The same view today.

89 The Methodist chapel was originally a corn store.

Mill Workers and Child Labour

Mill work was extremely unpleasant. A spokesman for Stockport factory workers described the conditions in 1831:

> The hours of labour in cotton mills are from 13 to 15 hours per day, and, at a distance from large towns, even longer. The rooms are artificially heated (to prevent the thread from breaking) from 60 to 90, and some 100 or 110 degrees, while those tropical atmospheres are impregnated with oily, gaseus, acid, and other noxious effluvia. At their labour there is no sitting, but the attention of children and females, the delicate and feeble, as well as the most healthy, must be as incessant as the revolutions of the machinery, for 6 or 7 hours before dinner and many more.

Apparently some factory workers remained cheerful despite their surroundings, a feat that earned the disapproval of at least one Manchester employer: 'Any hand in the mill seen talking to another, whistling, or singing, will be fined sixpence'.

In Greg's time children were seen as a source of cheap labour and it was legal to employ them in factories once they reached the age of seven. However without a Factories Act or Inspectors, it was not unusual for four-year-olds to be taken into employment. The majority of these children came from orphanages or poor houses where they had been a financial burden on parish funds. Indentures were signed, committing apprentices to work for the employer until they reach the age of 18, the employer agreeing to 'feed, clothe and educate' the children.

90 This drawing shows children collecting their pay. The scene would have been similar at Quarry Bank Mill.

91 Poor children queue to receive a warm meal.

The Apprentices' House

Although conditions were less harsh at Quarry Bank Mill, life for the child apprentice there could not be described as pleasant. Samuel Greg would only employ children aged nine years and older as they could work harder for longer periods. He preferred to employ girls as they were 'more adept with their fingers', and of course, by law, it was only boys who had to be educated. In 1790 Samuel Greg built the Apprentice House to accommodate these child labourers. Up to one hundred children lived here, supervised by Mr. and Mrs. Shawcross, who had their own apartment in the house.

Work began at 6 a.m. and finished 14 hours later. A 10-minute break was allowed for a breakfast of milk-porridge and water, whilst half an hour was set aside for a lunch of potatoes and bacon, taken at the Apprentices' House. Each day the apprentices at Styal would walk many miles, following the spinning mules back and forth, watching out for a broken yarn thread. The smaller apprentices would spend all day under the moving machinery, picking up cotton fluff to reduce the possibility of fires. During the lunch break, some children would be put to work dismantling and oiling machinery.

92 The Apprentices' House at Styal. In 1987 restoration commenced to return both internal and external features to how they would have appeared in 1830, when over 100 apprentices lived here. The house is now part of Quarry Bank Mill Museum and is open to visitors, although on Mondays it can be booked by school parties and pupils can re-enact the life of an apprentice.

Despite the rural surroundings, life at Quarry Bank Mill was not exactly healthy. The cotton lint would inflame the eyes of these children. Deafness was common, as was lung disease, and cancer from the machine oil. Many had fingers severed, and it has been recorded that in the first 20 years of the mill's existence 17 children were killed.

For their toil and trouble, apprentices were paid up to one shilling per week. However, for misdemeanours such as scrumping an apple, a fine of five shillings was imposed.

At the end of the day at the mill, the boys were given jobs in the garden whilst the girls would be kept busy sewing and darning. On Sunday mornings, the children would take what is known as 'The Apprentices Walk' from Styal to Wilmslow church, wearing their 'uniform'. This helped to identify any apprentice who tried to abscond. With a price on their head they were quickly returned to their employer, and punished by having all their hair removed (both boys and girls) and placed in solitary confinement.

The Apprentices' House has now been restored to the condition in which it would have appeared in 1830.

93 An apprentice's indenture, dated 1796.

94 Reconstruction of a room occupied by Mr. and Mrs. Shawcross.

95 It was in this classroom that apprentices would learn their 3 'R's. As early as 1788, John Thornton was paid 11s. 4d. a month for 'schooling' the apprentices on Sunday afternoons.

96 Two to a bed in these small dormitories.

97 The medical room in the Apprentices' House was pretty frugal. Notice the apprentices' capes hanging in the corner.

98 An 1830s reconstruction of the kitchen in the Apprentices' House.

99 This water pump stands outside the Apprentices' House, and would have been used by the children for washing and drinking.

Oak School

As early as 1788 John Thornton was paid 11s. 4d. per month for 'schooling' the apprentices on Sunday afternoons; the three 'R's were taught.

There was also a need to educate the children of the millworkers and so in 1823 Oak School was built onto the end of Oak Cottages. This was 10 years before the introduction of the Factory Act which made two hours' education a day compulsory for children under thirteen. Taught by the Greg family and itinerant teachers, young children attended Oak School during the day and the older ones at night. Apprentices attended in groups of eight for one evening a week.

The school remains in use today.

100   Pupils at Oak Village School, *c*.1910.

101 Pupils at Oak Village School in 1924.

Work and Play

102 In 1790 George Venables became one of the first migrant apprentices to start work at Quarry Bank Mill. His descendants continue to work at the mill and some still live in the village today. This photograph, taken at the turn of the century, shows Thomas Venables and his wife Elizabeth Ann *(centre)* and their family. Thomas was employed as a mechanic and was the great-grandson of George.

103 An earlier photograph, *c.*1880s, of Thomas Venables (born 1863) and his wife, Elizabeth Ann (née Worth).

104 William Folden, a gardener for the Gregs.

105 Albert Wright, who was employed as joiner, cabinet maker and undertaker.

106 Mill workers at Quarry Bank, *c*.1900

107 Quarry Bank Mill workers, *c*.1890. Notice that, with one exception, they followed the tradition of wearing hats at work.

108 A family gathering in their Sunday best. Oak Cottages can be seen in the background.

109 Carnivals were held regularly in the village. This photograph was taken in 1933.

110 Styal carnival in 1933. Miss Mollest, the headteacher of Styal School, can be seen in the centre of the front row.

111 The *Ship Inn*, still standing, is part of the estate. This photograph was taken in 1905.

Ringway and Manchester International Airport

Since Orville and Wilbur Wright's remarkable 59-second flight at Kitty Hawk on 7 December 1903, travel by aeroplane has developed in leaps and bounds. On what was, in those days, Firtree Farm now stands Terminal One of Manchester International Airport, and parts of Clough Bank, Ringway Woods, Oversley Farm and Oversley Lodge Farm are now covered in concrete.

In the early 1930s the company Norman Muntz & Dawbarn, aeronautical consultants, were asked by Manchester Corporation to examine the site and to submit proposals for extending the municipal airport at Barton Moss (near Barton bridge on the M63) to 'enable the Airport to fulfil modern commercial and continental requirements'.Their report concluded that 'owing to soil and meteorological conditions in the area, the creation of a first-class terminal airport at Barton Moss would be a matter of difficulty and expense so great that the question of moving the airport to another site must receive consideration'. It was believed that nothing larger than the planes already using Barton Moss Airport, such as the Douglas DC-2, would ever be able to land there. An investigation of alternative sites was carried out, including Wythenshawe and Woodford, but a general examination showed that the construction of a major airport would be possible at Ringway.

At this time the Fairey Aviation Company were manufacturing 'Battle' planes at their Heaton Chapel factory in Stockport, and in June 1937 they opened a new aircraft hanger at Ringway, where the final assembly and test flying of the plane were to be carried out. These single-engined bombers were fitted with Rolls Royce engines and carried one pilot, a rear gunner and an observer, whose job it was to aim the bombs by means of a special sight. By May 1939, some 53 aircraft each month were being produced for the R.A.F. as well as for both the Canadian and Australian Air Forces. Fairey continued to assemble and to test military aircraft at Ringway until the company's collapse in 1977.

Also A.V. Roe & Co. Ltd. were manufacturing a twin-engined long range bomber called 'The Anson' at Newton Heath in Manchester, before final assembly and testing at Woodford. They also had a small assembly plant at Ringway before and during the war, and a prototype of their 'Manchester' bomber flew from here on 24 July 1939, to be followed by many Lancasters.

The decision to build a new airport at Ringway was taken in July 1934, much to the consternation of local people who felt that an airport owned by Manchester Corporation should be in Manchester and not in rural Cheshire. This friction continues today, with complaints about noise and pollution, and the threat of more green belt land being swallowed up by the construction of a second main runway.

The airport was officially opened by the Secretary of State for Air, Sir Kingsley Wood, on 25 June 1938, and the first airlines to offer scheduled flights were the Dutch airline K.L.M. and the Isle of Man Services. By August 1939, 7,600 passengers had used the airport, sufficient to prove its viability.

The airport remained under the control of Manchester Corporation even during the Second World War, when Hurricanes and Spitfires were based here for the defence of the city.

After the war, commercial operations were resumed, the first service being Air France's Dakota to Paris on 17 April 1946. The airport became inter-continental in 1953 when Sabena commenced its transatlantic service to New York. The first 'Jumbo Jet' landed at Ringway in August 1970, followed by Concorde in November 1976.

From the airport's early beginnings, Ringway has increased dramatically. Runways have been extended, hotels and car parks built, and we have recently seen the opening of a second passenger terminal and a rail link from the centre of Manchester. Following local government reorganisation in 1974, the airport came under the control of Manchester Airport Joint Committee, and was renamed Manchester International Airport.

Ringway handled 10,000 passengers in 1946, 2,418,000 in 1974 and in 1991 an incredible 10,868,993. With around 130,000 air transport movements to 156 destinations each year, Manchester International Airport has now developed into the United Kingdom's third largest airport.

PROGRAMME

OF THE

OFFICIAL OPENING

OF THE

MANCHESTER (RINGWAY) AIRPORT

BY

His Majesty's Secretary of State
for Air

(*The Right Honourable Sir Kingsley Wood, P.C., M.P.*)

AND THEREAFTER AN

AIR DISPLAY

BY THE

ROYAL AIR FORCE

AND OTHERS

Saturday, 25th June, 1938

All communications with reference to the Air Display, to be addressed to :—

The Airport Manager, Manchester (Ringway) Airport, Yewtree Lane, Ringway, Cheshire.

112 The cover page for the official opening of Manchester Airport in 1938.

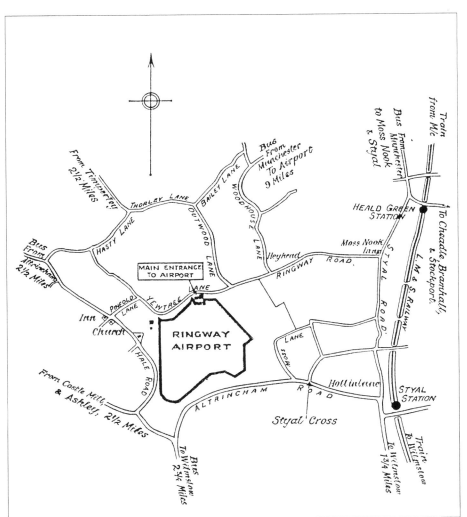

The map shows labels:

FROM TIMPERLEY 2½ MILES

THORLEY LANE

BAILEY LANE

WOODHOUSE LANE

BUS FROM MANCHESTER TO AIRPORT 9 MILES

Train from M/c

Bus from Manchester to Moss Nook & Styal

HEALD GREEN STATION

To Cheadle, Bramhall, & Stockport

OUTWOOD LANE

HASTY LANE

Moss Nook lane

Ileyhead

L.M & S RAILWAY

BUS FROM Altrincham 2½ MILES

MAIN ENTRANCE TO AIRPORT

RINGWAY ROAD

STYAL ROAD

PINFOLD LANE

LANE

YEWTREE LANE

Inn

Church

RINGWAY AIRPORT

LANE SNOW

HALE ROAD

Hollinlane

STYAL STATION

FROM Castle Mill & Ashley, 2½ MILES

ALTRINCHAM ROAD

Styal Cross

To Wilmstow 1¾ Miles

Train to Wilmstow

Bus To Wilmslow 2¾ Miles

113 The best site for Manchester airport, as suggested by aeronautical consultants Norman Muntz and Dawbarn.

114 Norman Muntz and Dawbarn's design for the terminal building.

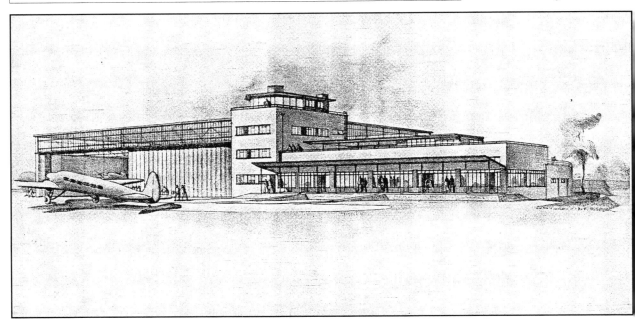

MANCHESTER (RINGWAY) AIRPORT
ENCLOSURE DIAGRAM

Manor Farm

From Altrincham

Pinfold Lane

The Grange

Fairey Aviation Co. Hangars

Church

ENTRANCE

Yewtree Lane

ENTRANCE TO PRIVATE ENCLOSURE

Ringway Road
To Manchester

M/c Corporation Hangar

Firtree Farm

PRIVATE ENCLOSURE

PUBLIC SEATING ENCLOSURE ONLY. NO CARS.

} ADMISSION 1/-

Newbridge House

ENTRANCE

FREE PUBLIC ENCLOSURE.

CARS 1/-

REFRESHMENT MARQUEES IN EACH ENCLOSURE

Cloughbank Farm

ENTRANCE

SEATING 1/-

ENTRANCE

Hale Road

**CARS 1/-
FREE PUBLIC ENCLOSURE**

SEATING 1/-

To Wilmslow

ENTRANCE

Higher Mainwood Farm

Altrincham Road

ENTRANCES

ENTRANCES

Oversley Lodge Farm

Oversley Lodge

Lower Mainwood Cottages

Oversley Farm

River Bollin

Lower Mainwood Farm

To Wilmslow

1000FT   500   0   1/4   1/2   3/4   1 Mile

115 A plan of the airport's enclosure in 1938.

TRAVEL IN COMFORT.

Manchester to the Continent
by
K.L.M. ROYAL DUTCH AIR LINES.

Daily service except Sundays. Opening date, June 27, 1938.

The service will be operated by Douglas DC2 (as illustrated) and Lockheed Super Electra machines, well known for their sound proof cabin and general comfort.

10.30		dep. . . Manchester . .		arr.	18.05
13.15		arr. . . Amsterdam . .		dep.	16.00
Fares : Single £5 5s.				Return £9 9s.

In Amsterdam through connections to Berlin, Copenhagen, Paris, Malmo, Prague, Vienna, Budapest, etc.

Further information may be obtained from the K.L.M. Office, Ringway Airport, Tel. : Gatley 3225 ; Messrs. Wm. H. Müller & Co. (London), Ltd., Victoria Buildings, St. Mary's Gate, Manchester, Tel. : Blackfriars 3000 ; and principal tourist agents.

116 An advertisement for KLM's flights to Amsterdam. It is interesting to note that flights which now take an hour took four times as long in 1938.

117 This advert for the Isle of Man Air Services appeared in the Official Opening Programme in 1938.

ISLE OF MAN AIR SERVICES
LIMITED

OPERATORS OF REGULAR SCHEDULED AIR SERVICES AND CONTRACTORS TO H.M. POST OFFICE FOR THE CONVEYANCE OF MAILS BY AIR

SERVICES OPERATED TO AND FROM

ISLE OF MAN · LIVERPOOL · BLACKPOOL
MANCHESTER · GLASGOW · CARLISLE
BELFAST · LEEDS · BRADFORD

RAIL AND STEAMER TICKETS INTERCHANGED

FULL DETAILS REGARDING TIMES, FARES, ETC., MAY BE OBTAINED AT ANY AIRPORT OFFICE, RAILWAY STATION, OR RECOGNISED TRAVEL AGENT

Head Office : Isle of Man Airport, Isle of Man   Branches at the above airports

Used for high-speed reconnaissance and bombing operations, large numbers of Avro Ansons are in service in the

Royal Air Force and in the Air Forces of Australia, Eire, Estonia, Finland and Egypt.

A. V. Roe & Co. Ltd., Newton Heath, MANCHESTER

Telephone COLlyhurst 2731

118 Advertisement for Avro Anson.

119 Soil removal during the construction of the airport.

120 The aircraft hanger at Ringway where the final assembly of the 'Battle' planes was carried out.

121 Taken on 26 June 1938, this photograph shows Sir Kingsley Wood, His Majesty's Secretary of State for Air, at the official opening of Ringway Airport.

122 The first aircraft in service was this Douglas DC2, operated by KLM from Manchester to Amsterdam.

123 One of KLM's Douglas DC2s at Ringway in the late 1930s. Is the man underneath the wing tip carrying the fuel?

124 Taken in 1938, this photograph shows a Dragon Rapide outside the original terminal building and control tower.

125 The restaurant pre-war.

126 A Whitley Bomber at Ringway, 1938.

127 In 1940 Churchill decided that 5,000 men should be trained as paratroopers. Early in July the first draft of 800 men arrived at Ringway where a hanger had been set aside for instructions in jumping and landing techniques.

128 & 129 (*Below and opposite*) Safety was of prime importance for these novice paratroopers. Here they are being shown how to fit and operate their parachutes.

130   Parachute packers at Ringway, *c.*1940. The notice behind them says 'Remember a man's life depends on every parachute you pack'.

131   For greater secrecy and better weather conditions, landing took place at Tatton Park whilst trial descents into water took place at Rostherne Mere. This photograph shows a parachutist landing safely in Tatton Park, *c.*1940.

132 Greetings to passengers on the Air France DC3 Dakota's inaugural Paris to Manchester flight on 17 April 1946.

133 This was the public entrance to the airport after the war. The building was originally part of the garrison building. This photograph dates from 1957.

134 *(Left)* On 9 October 1962 Prince Philip opened the new international departure extension at Manchester Airport. The building became renowned for its magnificent chandeliers as well as the bronze statue commemorating the Wright brothers' first flight and the stained glass window dedicated to the wartime paratroopers.

135 *(Above)* The 50th anniversary of Manchester Airport was commemorated by a march of the Parachute Regiment led by their mascot *Pegasus*.

136 British Airways Concorde stands in the Manchester rain, *c*.1982.

Alderley Edge Village

With many exclusive, individually-designed properties set in wooded landscape, and within easy reach of motorways, mainline stations, and Manchester Airport, Alderley Edge remains one of the most affluent and prestigious residential areas in the North West.

The 'village' of Alderley Edge gets its name from the nearby sandstone outcrop of the Pennines. Originally the area was known as Chorley, but was renamed in 1894. It is often confused with the ancient townships of Nether and Over Alderley which lie a few miles along the Congleton Road.

Little has changed in the last 70 years when Charles Prince wrote the following:

London Road, the principal street of the village, is considered to be one of the prettiest village thoroughfares in the kingdom. It is 61ft wide and planted on both sides with trees. Numerous modern fine buildings are noticed, amongst which are the three banks (The Union Bank of Manchester, The Manchester & Liverpool District Bank and Williams Deacons Bank), the Public Hall and Union Club, the Church Institute and the St Hilary's Schools. Many high-class shops are here, and the General Post Office is at the foot of the hill at the southern end of the village.

TELEPHONE 137.

BURNS & RIDGWAY,

COAL, COKE, LIME, AND GRAVEL MERCHANTS,

CARTING CONTRACTORS,

STATION YARD, ALDERLEY EDGE.

Manures :: Potting Sods :: Sand :: Patent Fire Lighters

---

137 In the 19th and early 20th centuries, coal was a very important commodity—for domestic heating, the manufacture of gas for street lighting and cooking, and to fuel the boilers of the mills. The quickest delivery from the coalfields of south Lancashire was by rail and Burns and Ridgway were quick to seize the opportunity of establishing coal distribution depots at both Wilmslow and Alderley Edge stations.

138 White's *Directory of Cheshire* for 1860 describes the *Queen's Hotel* as a spacious and commodious building, comfortably fitted up, and affording every accommodation to visitors. This advertisement for the *Queen's Hotel* appeared in 1923.

TELEPHONE 9 ALDERLEY. GARAGE.

QUEEN'S HOTEL :
Alderley Edge.

This old-established Family and Residential Hotel has recently undergone complete alterations and decorations, is comfortably and admirably situated near the Station in the loveliest part of Cheshire, within half-hour of Manchester; near Golf Links.

Special Terms for Families, Boarders, and Week-ends.

Weddings and Picnics catered for.

Alderley Edge Bakery.

ESTABLISHED 1880.

Motor deliveries daily to all parts of the district.

GEORGE CRAGG,

BAKER,

Brown Street, Alderley Edge.

My Three Points :

Quality :: Purity :: Civility

---

139 (*Above left*) A 1923 advertisement for a bakery.

---

140 (*Above right*) A 1923 advertisement for G.W. Broadbent, house furnisher and funeral director.

141 (*Left*) Advertisements dating from 1923 for plumbers, florists and a tea room.

142 Who could believe that this pastoral scene of Wilmslow Road, taken early this century, is now a section of the A34, with its constant flow of cars and lorries?

143 The *Trafford Arms* was a very ancient inn, but was entirely rebuilt in 1859, the coat of arms of the Trafford family being incorporated into the gable end. This photograph shows the *Trafford Arms Hotel*, as it became known, in 1897. The low white house on the left was the toll house.

144 This undated postcard shows the *Trafford Arms* and Congleton Road.

145 & 146 Apart from the absence of cars, these two photographs could have been taken in the village yesterday. In fact the first one was taken towards the end of the last century whilst the second was taken in the early 1900s.

147 St Hilary's school stands at the junction of Congleton Road and Macclesfield Road and was founded some time before 1880 to meet the demand for 'middle-class' education. Originally it was intended to cater for the educational needs of around 330 girls, a number that remains the same today. Part of the old building was demolished in 1977 to make way for a sports hall. These photographs show the school before and during demolition.

148 This pastoral scene of London Road was probably taken in the 1880s. Alderley Edge station is on the left.

149 As with Wilmslow, it was the building of the railways that had the greatest affect on the population, and, to cater for the new commuters, the railway company erected the *Queen's Hotel*, adjoining what was then known as Alderley and Chorley station. Opened in 1844, the hotel had a frontage of over 300ft. and contained 70 rooms.

150 Alderley Edge station. When first opened in 1843 the train journey from Alderley to London took 10½ hours.

151 No. 48269 arrives at Alderley Edge station on 29 August 1957.

152 Waiting for a train at Alderley Edge station.

St Philip's church

It was not until the middle of the 19th century that the village of Chorley obtained a church of its own, the nearest being St Mary's in 'Old Alderley' as Nether and Over Alderley were beginning to be called. Standing on the corner of Wilmslow Road and Ryleys Lane, the church was built in the Gothic style in 1852. The 175ft.-spire has been described as 'the most graceful and best proportioned in Cheshire'. Covering the wall at the back of the altar is a beautifully carved ornamental screen. Known as a 'reredos', it is thought to be of Tyrolean origin, dating from 1903.

153 This old photograph, taken from the corner of Wilmslow Road and Ryleys Lane, shows St Philip's church and the village post office.

154 A recent photograph of St Philip's.

155 The Rev. James Whitworth Consterdine M.A. of Trinity College, Cambridge, became the first incumbent at St Philip's church. His salary of £360 per annum was paid from pew rents. Originally there were 500 seats within the church, of which 200 were free.

156 The interior of St Philip's church.

157 The carved reredos.

Chorley Hall

Possibly the oldest inhabited house in Cheshire, it is believed that Chorley Hall was first built in 1330 as a single-storied hall with a two-storied wing at the eastern end and a central fireplace. Some of the original features remain, including the doorways of the through passage and the three doorways that led off this passageway to the buttery, the pantry and the kitchen. The old stone bridge across the moat also still stands.

Around 1560 the Davenport family made substantial changes to the building. The roof of the Hall was raised in order to insert a second floor. The central fireplace was replaced by a wall fireplace, and a stairway built next to it.

It was at this time that the two-storey black-and-white timber building was erected. Initially it was not connected to the older building, this being carried out in the last century when a brick staircase block was added.

One of the rooms in the 16th-century building contains a finely carved black oak chimney-piece on which is inscribed:

Such were the rooms in which of yore
Our ancestors were wont to dwell;
And still the fashion knows no more
These lingering relics tell.

The oaken wainscot richly graced
With gay festoons of mimic flowers;
The armorial bearings now defaced,
All speak of proud and long passed hours.

158 This photograph of Chorley Hall was taken some time before 1870.

159 The south front of Chorley Hall, 1993.

The Edge

This red sandstone escarpment, some 1,000 ft. thick, was created 200 million years ago at the bottom of the ocean. Now rising to a height of over 500 ft. above the Cheshire Plain, it was forced upwards at a time when the earth's crust was less stable than it is today. Yet few of the thousands of annual visitors who come to this wooded hillside for a stroll or a picnic and to observe the spectacular views are aware of its long and strange past.

It is believed that the area has been mined for copper since prehistoric times, and excavations in the last century disturbed much older workings in which roughly made stone hammers of local rock were found. These have been variously dated to the Bronze Age and Roman period.

Bronze-Age stone shafthole axes and a cremation urn containing remains from the Early Bronze Age have also been found and, in 1974, four Roman coins showing the heads of Elgabus, Postumus, Crispus and Valentinian I were discovered.

In December 1745, Bonnie Prince Charlie's army marched over the Edge on their way to Macclesfield and beyond. They would have found the place a dreary and desolate common, for it was only earlier that year that Sir James and Sir Edward Stanley began to plant the hundreds of fir trees that now cover the area.

In 1779 the common was enclosed, together with other waste land in Alderley, and remained in the Lord of the Manor's possession until 1933, when part of the Wizard Wood was purchased by the Urban District Council in trust for preservation. Five years later and following a compulsory order, The Edge was sold by the Alderley Estates to the Urban District Council, who handed it over to the National Trust in 1947.

160 Macclesfield Road which leads from the village to the Edge.

161 The Edge viewed from the north, showing Hough Lane with Mottram Lane in front. This photograph dates from the turn of the century.

162 This photograph was taken by Mr. W. Greenwood and shows a collection of stone hammers that were found at Alderley Edge. They can now be seen at Manchester University Museum.

163 Copper mining at Alderley Edge.

164 The beacon at Alderley Edge at
the turn of the century. Built in 1799,
it was blown down in a gale in 1931.

The Beacon

The Beacon is the highest point on the Edge and is shown on the maps of Cheshire produced by both Saxton in 1577 and Speed in 1610. At this period it would have been visible for many miles around. Originally it was surmounted by a 'hollow square room with a door, and having an iron pot kept in it for the purpose of holding pitch and tar, ready to light in times of threatened attack'. In 1588 a beacon blazed from this point to warn that the Spanish Armada had been sighted off Cornwall.

In 1799, at a time when England was at war with France, the building was replaced. A description of it is given by Charles Prince:

> [The Beacon] Is an oblong, rectangular building, about 12 feet long by six feet broad, and about twenty feet high, and is built of stone and brick. The height of the square portion is about twelve feet, and is composed of heavy blocks of stone; this is surmounted by a brick pyramid.

165 A hundred yards or so from the beacon stands Castle Rock, from which extensive views of the northern Cheshire plain towards Rivington Pike and Blackstone Edge can be seen. Although traces of the foundation of a fortress dating from the 17th century have been found in the field behind the Rock, it is thought that it was never completed, a site at Beeston, 22 miles away, being preferred. The place was apparently used as a lookout station during the Civil War, and, whilst digging a ditch near the rock around 1769, an old resident named Thomas Ridgeway uncovered parcels of gun flints.

Wizard's Well

Continuing in a north-westerly direction from Castle Rock, the path eventually arrives at the Wizard's Well, formed by a natural spring. Above the well, carved in the rock, is the face of the wizard and the inscription:

Drink of this and take thy fill
For the water falls by the Wizard's will

The wizard is reputed to be Merlin, of Arthurian fame, and relates to a curious legend first published in 1805 as *The Iron Gate*.

Two iron gates with bolt and lock,
With welded bars and grid,
Somewhere beneath the castle rock*
'Tis said have long been hid.

Concealed by heather or by furze,
The place remains unknown
Whether beneath the seven firs*
Or near the golden stone.

Some say they're by the Miners' Arms, [1]
Some say higher up the hill,
By Stormy Point* or Leighton's farms,
In short—they're where you will.

If peradventure, Samuel Bratt,
Or old John Bratt[2] should say,
They at Monks Heath deny him flat,
His gates are blown away.

But where they are? what matters it,
Compared with what's behind,
Where many a noble gallant tit,
Has long been kept confined.

Except at times on windy nights,
Strange glimmering forms they say
Are seen to take their airy flights,
And horses heard to neigh.

Neer heed the men, we've them e' now,
True British hearts and stout,
Give us the tits and we will show
How we can ride them out.

Let Government remit the tax
And open wide the gate,
Brave Alderley, upon their backs,
Will soon be all agait.

And if we find them sound and good,
We'll groom them at the Hagg[3]
Or billet them in Clock House Wood,*
Below with Thomas Cragg,

And England's King and Britain's land
Shall look in vain to see,
When danger's near, a nobler band
To fight for Alderley.

And troops of men in black they tell,
Entoomed in cavern deep,
Far underneath the holy well*
For years and ages sleep.

* Places on Alderley Edge. 1. *The Wizard Inn*; 2. Landlord of *The Iron Gates Inn*, Monks Heath. The sign of the inn had been blown down; 3. Now the Mine's House.

166 *(Below left)* The Wizard's Well.

167 *(Below right)* Is this the face of Merlin? The face of the wizard has been engraved into the rock above his well. Below his face can be seen the inscription.

168 This photograph was taken between 1880 and 1890 when the *Wizard Inn* was known as *The Miners Arms*. For several generations it was kept as a fully-licensed house. Whether it was due to excessive 'quenching of thirsts' by the miners is unknown, but at the beginning of this century the licence lapsed and it became a temperance house.

169 Near the *Wizard Inn* is the 'Engine Vein', site of the largest of the mines at Alderley. Veins of copper, iron, and lead have been found in the sandstone here.

Stormy Point

There sullen woods—here barren fells,
On Stormy Point the eye now dwells;
No loveliness herself hath she,
But from her heights, you grandeur see:
Look right, look left, look straight away,
The time so spent, the look will pay.

J.Ditton
(pre-1923)

Stormy Point stands some 600 ft. above sea level, affording views of the Yorkshire and Derbyshire Hills. Lyme Cage, situated in Lyme Park, near Disley, is very conspicuous, whilst in the foreground will be noticed Mottram St Andrews and Mottram Common. Immediately below Stormy Point is Dickens Wood with Waterfall Woods and the Clockhouse Woods receding into the distance on the right.

It is said that local people hid their cattle and possessions in the ravine of Waterfall Woods, to protect them from the Jacobite army which passed along Macclesfield Road in December 1745.

170 This entrance to old mines can be found at Stormy Point.

171 A popular haunt for visitors, the views from Stormy Point are spectacular.

Alderley Cross

The ancient Cross, itself scarce seen
So shaded by a hawthorn green;
And near it still an old friend stands,
And guides our way with outstretched hands,
Time worn are both, but what their age,
No record tell, nor village sage.

Chas. H. Prince (1923)

Broken by Cromwellians during the Civil War, the cross once stood in the centre of this crossroad, but was moved to the side to protect it from the heavy traffic that travels along the A34.

It is thought that wandering friars preached here in the Middle Ages. Until recently a market was held at Alderley Cross every Saturday.

The hawthorn, which still grows around the base, is reputed to have been taken from the Glastonbury Thorn which grew from the staff of Joseph of Arimathea, itself cut from the tree that blossomed at the nativity.

172 & 173 Facing the *Wizard Inn* is a lane known as 'Welsh Row' or 'Artists Lane' in which some of the oldest black and white cottages in the neighbourhood are to be found.

174 This junction of Welsh Row and Congleton Road is known locally as 'Cross Brow'. This undated photograph shows a group of men with their backs to the cross, idly observing the scene at what is now the busy A34.

175 The stump of Alderley Cross now stands at the side of the main road.

Old Alderley

Here's health to the Alderley lasses,
The dark and the fair and the brown,
Come lads, fill up quickly your glasses,
Here's to each you love best in the town.

Not forgetting the lasses in Warford
The growing as well as the grown
May they find wheresoever is offered
A hand and a heart like their own.

c.1839

A mile or so south of Alderley Edge, on the A34 Congleton Road, lie Nether Alderley, Over Alderley and Great Warford, and together these 'townships' made up the ancient parish of Alderley.

To save confusion with the modern town of Alderley Edge, Nether and Over Alderley are often referred to as 'Old Alderley'. They are both mentioned in Domesday Book, their respective entries being:

ALDERLEY. Godwin held it as free man. 1 hide paying tax.
Land for 8 ploughs. In lordship 1, with 2 ploughmen;
3 villagers and 1 rider with 1 plough.
Meadow, 1 acre; woodland 1½ leagues long and 1 league wide;
2 enclosures.
Value before 1066, 20s; now 10s; found waste.

William holds Alderley from the Earl. Brown held it. He was a
free man. 1 hide paying tax. Land for 4 ploughs.
It was and is waste.
Woodland 2 leagues long and 2 wide.
Value before 1066, 20s.

Mr William Webb, writing in 1621, gave the following description of the area:

... we came to *Alderleigh*, where we behold afar off both the Parish Church, and near to it a very gallant house and seat of the *Standleys* [sic], derived from the Honourable discent [sic] of the Earls of Derby, late the possession of Sir *Tho. Stanley*, Knight, of much esteem, and now of *Tho. Stanley*, Esquire, his heir (i); a man like to uphold the worthy accompt of his Ancestors. More conspicuous is this place, by the Beacon mounted upon an eminent Hill over the Town (ii). A devise [sic], which in that and other high places in all Counties of *England* used in times past, and may be again, if God be not more mercifull [sic] then [sic] we deserve, to great purpose, in time of invasion and insurrection.

(i) Sir Thomas Stanley, Knt., died Nov. 21 1606. This Thomas Stanley, Esq., was not created a Baronet till 25 June 1660.

(ii) This is the Beacon on Alderley Edge.

Alderley Hall

Alderley Hall, the residence of the Stanleys, stood close to Nether Alderley Mill. Surrounded by a moat which could be crossed by a stone bridge of two arches, the hall commanded extensive views of Alderley Park, the ancient parish church, and the plain of Cheshire. A stone-arched gateway, close to the road, was built by Sir Thomas Stanley (1597-1672), the first of the Stanley family to inherit the Alderley Manors. It was Sir Thomas who planted the beech wood by Radnore Mere.

In the spring of 1779, following a fire which destroyed Alderley Hall, the Stanleys moved to Park House. This was demolished in 1818 and a new Park House was built on the same site. The house had 40 principal bedrooms and six large halls, together with a brewery, mill house, laundry and home farm.

Pigot's *Commercial Directory* for 1834 says that

> Alderley Park, the seat of Sir J.T. Stanley Bart., who is Lord of the Manor, is of some considerable extent, beautifully wooded, and boasts some of the largest beech trees in the country. The scenery from all parts of this domain is rich and beautiful, considerably heightened by the fine sheet of water called Radnor Mere.

In 1931 Park House met the fate of the original Alderley Hall and the Stanley family moved into the Tenants Hall. Built in 1819 as a ballroom, it obtained its name from the annual Christmas party held there for the tenants and their families.

After the break up of the family estate in 1938, the park site was purchased by a property developer. Unfortunately, the war put paid to his plans and Alderley Park fell into disrepair.

After the war, Britain's largest chemical company, I.C.I., purchased the site for £55,000 with the intention of using it as an attractive new research site to reverse the 'brain drain' and attract world-class scientists.

Following the recent division of I.C.I.'s operations, their Pharmaceutical Division has become part of Zeneca who currently employ over 3,000 people at Alderley Park. Many of the old buildings remain, including the coach house and stables, now used as a training centre, and the grain store, now the *Stanley Arms*.

176 This drawing shows Alderley Hall before the disastrous fire in 1779.

177 An undated postcard of Alderley Hall.

Nether Alderley Mill

Standing on the east side of Congleton Road, this 16th-century water mill was built to grind the corn for the Nether Alderley Estate, home of the Stanley family. It continued in operation until 1939, the last miller being Mr. Rawlins. After the war it was presented to the National Trust and, although a great deal of restoration was necessary, including that on the 19th-century machinery, the internal posts and roof-framing are contemporary.

These timbers were numbered by the Elizabethan carpenters, and it would appear that the frames were assembled on the ground before being placed *in situ*.

The millwrights used the back wall of the mill to dam a small stream, thereby producing sufficient water to keep the mill in operation for eight hours a day. Radnore Mere was also excavated in the grounds of Nether Alderley Hall to provide an additional water supply in times of drought.

178 *(Above)* Nether Alderley Mill with the kiln, now demolished, on the right of the picture. This rare photograph was supplied by Brian Hobson who can be seen on the extreme left.

179 *(Right)* Between Alderley Cross and the mill, on the east side of Congleton Road, is a lane on which stands The Mill House. Like the Smithy Cottage next door, it was built in 1912 as an Estate House and is adorned by the Stanleys' coat of arms 'The Eagle and Child'.

180 & 181 The 'Smithy Cottage' occupies the site of the blacksmith's shop, shown here in these two undated photographs.

182 Facing 'Smithy Cottage' is Nether Alderley County Primary School, known earlier this century as the County Council Day School. This low, brick building was erected and endowed by the Hon. Miss Jane Stanley, of Alderley, in 1822, although considerable additions have been made since then.

83 Almost opposite Nether Alderley Mill is a black-and-white farm building dated 1688. This was formerly the village inn, known as *The Eagle and Child* or, as the locals called it, *The Brid and the Babby*. The inn is on the left of this undated photograph whilst in the centre there are a number of cottages, one of which was the village shop.

184 The farmhouse today.

185 The path by these cottages leads to St Mary's church.

Alderley church

Hidden from the main road, yet only a few yards down a lane opposite Nether Alderley Mill, lies one of Cheshire's gems, St Mary's church.

The church, originally dedicated to St Lawrence, patron saint of cooks, dates from the 13th century, the first rector being Robert Byron who died in 1328. With few exceptions, little of·the medieval fabric remains.

The redstone tower, which measures 23ft. 6ins. from east to west and 22ft. 6ins. from north to south, was built during the reign of Henry VII whose shield of arms, 'three lions passant guardant', can be seen on the summit. The doorway on the west side is decorated with 14th-century mouldings.

Careful examination of the tower shows damage from musket shots. As to whether the tower was used for target practice or whether fighting took place here during the Civil War, one can only speculate.

The tower contains six bells, bearing the inscriptions:

1. Come away, make no delay, 1787
2. blank
3. Prosperity to this parish, 1787
4. This peal was cast at Gloucester by C. & J. Rudhall, 1787
5. C. & J. Mears, Foundry, London. Parish of Alderley, August 23, 1847
6. I to the church the living call and to the grave do summon all, 1787

In 1577 the manor of Nether Alderley was purchased from Thomas Stanley by Sir Edward Fitton of Gawsworth Hall. The Fittons then proceeded to remove the Stanleys' private chapel, resulting in legal disputes between the families. The right to a private chapel was eventually granted to the Stanleys in 1591, and an elaborate Jacobean gallery pew was made, reckoned to be one of the finest of its kind in the country and unique to Cheshire. In order that the two families did not meet, access to the pew could only be gained from the flight of steps on the outside of the church.

In 1851 the chancel was destroyed, and in 1877 the church underwent drastic restoration in which the square pews were removed, the floor of the church was restored to its former level, and the old roof revealed by the removal of the plaster ceiling.

The churchyard contains many interesting tombstones, including that of the village blacksmith, John Henshall, who died on 25 September 1814, aged 77.

My sledge and hammer lie declined,
My bellows, too, have lost their wind;
My fire's extinct, my force decayed,
My vice is in the dust all laid.
My coal is spent, my iron gone,
My nails are drove, my work is done.
My fire-dried corpse lies here to rest,
My smoke-like soul soars to the blest.

The churchyard did not escape the ghoulish trade of the grave robbers, and in his book, *Old Cheshire Churches*, Raymond Richards records the following events:

Early last century resurrectionists are known to have carried on their ghoulish calling in Alderley churchyard. In October 1830, body-snatchers exhumed the newly interred bodies of two women, one of Great Warford, and the other a young girl of sixteen, formerly of Stockport. Fortunately, two of the men engaged in this gruesome trade were caught. When brought up for trial, it was found that the statute book of 1830 contained no law against body snatching, and the only charge possible was that of trespass and stealing the dead women's wedding ring. For a long time afterwards the parishioners of Alderley kept silent watch in turns over the little graveyard, and placed great stones from the quarry in the middle of all newly opened graves. To this day huge stones are dug up by the sexton when re-opening graves in the older part of the churchyard.

186   Alderley church, as it appeared before the restoration of 1877.

187 A drawing of Alderley church from the beginning of the 19th century.

188 By the church gate is this picturesque stone building, built as a school in 1628 and referred to by Charles Dickens in his *Old Curiosity Shop*.

189 In 1700 the Bishop of Chester, Francis Gastrell, described the school building in his 'Notitia Cestriensis', saying that 'the room below was to teach and another above was for ye master to lodge in'. At this time the master's salary would have been about £12 per annum.

190 In 1909 the school building was restored by the Rt. Hon. E.C. Stanley, fourth Baron Stanley of Alderley, who had also assumed the title 'Lord Sheffield'. He presented it to the parish council for use as a parish hall. At the same time he ordered the construction of this mausoleum which now dominates the churchyard.

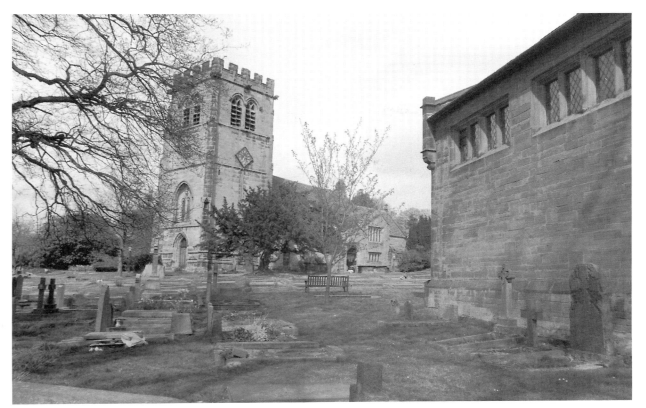

191 St Mary's church with the Stanley mausoleum on the right.

192 The Jacobean gallery pew, built by the Stanleys in the 16th century.

193 The only entrance to the Stanley pew is via these external steps.

194 A curiosity of St Mary's church are these grooves worn into the walls of the south porch when villagers sharpened their arrows here.

195 Within the churchyard stands this stump of an ancient churchyard cross, having been cut down through Puritan zeal following an Act of Parliament which required all such crosses to be reduced to a standard size. In 1700 the churchwardens paid 14s. 10d. for a new brass sundial. It surmounted the stump of the cross and bore the inscription *Umbram dum spectas refugit revolubile tempus, 1700,* (whilst thou lookest at the shadow, fleeting time is gone). The sundial was recently stolen.

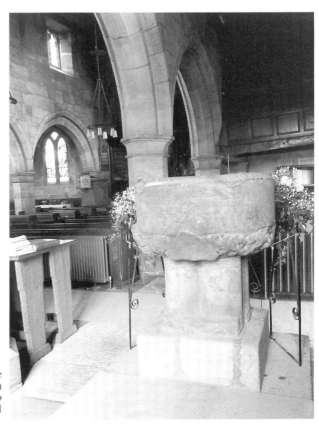

196 In 1821 this old font was discovered buried at the side of the churchyard. It is thought to have been made in the 14th century and was hidden in the times of the Commonwealth to prevent its destruction. It has now been restored to its original use.

Bibliography

Aiken, J., *A description of the County from thirty to forty miles around Manchester* (1795)

Bagshaw's *Directory of Cheshire* (1850)

Bee, M., *Industrial Revolution and Social Reform in the Manchester Region* (1984)

Bradshaw, L.D., *Visitors to Manchester c.1538-1865* (1987)

Boucher, Cyril T.E., *Nether Alderley Mill* (1974)

Chetham Society, *Wills and Inventories* (1857)

Crossley, *A guide to Alderley Edge* (1931)

Dictionary of National Biography (Oxford University Press)

Earwaker, J.P., *East Cheshire Past and Present* (vols. 1 & 2), (1877)

Jeuda, Basil, *Railways of the Macclesfield District* (1984)

Kelly's *Directory of Cheshire* (1892)

Kelly's *Directory of Cheshire* (1906)

Kelly's *Directory of Cheshire* (1928)

Morris's *Directory of Cheshire* (1874)

Pigot & Co., *Commercial Directory for the County of Cheshire* (1834)

Parish of Alderley Edge—The Official Guide (1977)

Prince, Chas. H., *Historical Guide to Alderley Edge* (1923)

Quarry Bank Mill Trust, *Teachers' Notes & Bibliography* (1984)

Railton, C.W. & Maltby, K.M., *The Story of Alderley Edge andd its Church* (undated)

Richards, R., *Old Cheshire Churches* (1947)

Seed's *Macclesfield and District Directory* (1910)

Stanhope-Brown, J., *Manchester to Styal via Swinton* (undated)

Tigwell, R.E., *Cheshire in the twentieth century*

Trades Union Congress, *The History of the T.U.C. 1868-1968* (1968)

Tunnicliffe, W., *A topographical survey of the Counties of Stafford, Chester, and Lancaster* (1787)

Victoria History of the County of Chester